Phonics Without Worksheets

Vowels

Written by

Carol Mader

Editor:

Alaska Hults

Illustrator:

Kate Flanagan

Project Director:

Carolea Williams

Special thanks to:
Celeste Johnson for her creative contributions and encouragement

CTP © 1999 Creative Teaching Press, Inc., Huntington Beach, CA 92649
Reproduction of activities in any manner for use in the classroom and not for commercial sale is permissible.
Reproduction of these materials for an entire school or for a school system is strictly prohibited.

Table of Contents

Introduction

The *Phonics Without Worksheets* series invites you to make phonics fun for your students through cooperative learning, hands-on craft-making, interactive games, and activities with multisensory appeal. *Vowels* is a resource book for teachers or any adults who help students learn to read. Rather than using a paper-and-pencil format, it features easy and quick-to-prepare games, crafts, and activities to help students learn the sounds (phonemes) of letters and letter combinations, providing a systematic, logical, sequential, and fun way to teach phonics. These activities complement any existing reading program.

Research shows that when learning involves more than one of the five senses students more readily acquire and retain information. *Vowels* encourages students to

- **hear** letters and words spoken and read.
- **see** letters and words in a variety of visual forms.
- **touch** and create letter-related crafts.
- **smell** food prepared to reinforce letter sounds.
- **taste** food prepared during the activities.

The activities in this resource incorporate a variety of methods to help you meet the needs of students with different learning styles. Many activities can be expanded to involve parents and enable them to share in the thrill of seeing their children blossom into readers. Students can apply their new knowledge right away while reading the mini-books—short stories with a repetitive presentation of specific vowels—and completing the suggested picture-card activities. Use your favorite children's literature to further extend your students' experiences with language and letters. Look for this symbol to find tips for quickly modifying activities when you are working with one student.

The *Phonics Without Worksheets* series involves students in their own learning by engaging their senses and emotions to bring meaning to their interactions with the sounds and images of language.

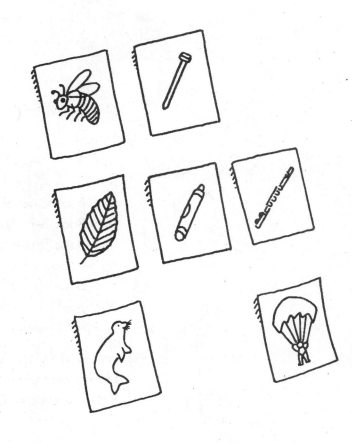

How to Use This Book

Use the sequenced activities presented in *Vowels* to create an organized phonics program in which students are taught to associate letters with letter sounds. These sounds are also called phonemes. To teach the phoneme activities in *Vowels*, read each activity ahead of time; gather the necessary materials; and make any modifications your teaching space, time, or resources might require. As you read the activities, note that a letter or group of letters contained within two slashes refers to the

sound a student hears—as in /short a/ for the vowel sound in *cat* and /long a/ in *gate*. *Vowels* is arranged so that short vowels are presented first and separates the somewhat similar vowel sounds of short *a* and short *e* by introducing the more distinctive sounds of short *i* and short *o* before presenting short *e*.

Sight words are those words that do not obey phonetic rules. They must be memorized as a whole word to be recognized by sight. For example, if read phonetically, *done* would be pronounced as if it rhymed with *bone*. If a student tries to spell it phonetically, he or she would spell it *dun*. Pages 7 and 8 contain hands-on activities that can be used to teach the sight words listed on page 8.

Mini-books (pages 58–63) are small reproducible books that provide repeated use of specific vowels. They are provided as an added reinforcement, and the accompanying review activities give students additional practice in working with the letters they are learning to use. The mini-books can be colored and assembled by students. See pages 56 and 57 for a variety of educational and enjoyable activities that incorporate the mini-books.

Picture cards (pages 67–80) with images of familiar objects whose names tend to be well-known by students are also included. Invite students to say aloud the name of the object on each picture card and listen for the sounds they hear in the name. Letter cards and activity ideas (pages 64–66) are provided for use with the picture cards to extend learning.

Here are some tips for incorporating this resource into your phonics program:

- *Anticipate*—Read each activity ahead of time to know what to expect. Encourage parents to donate any materials your class might need.

- *Brainstorm*—When introducing a new phoneme, write the letter(s) on the board and tell students what sound it makes. Ask students to name words that include this phoneme. Write their suggestions on the board, and discuss words they suggest that do not have that phoneme—students learn from these attempts, too. If students get stuck, write consonants across the board. Blend the consonant with the vowel and challenge students to think of a word that starts with that consonant-vowel blend.

- *Read and Speak*—The sooner students can apply their knowledge of phonemes by seeing the letters in print and hearing them read by you, the better they'll retain the information. Invite students to locate specific letter sounds in stories, poems, and songs. Also, verbally emphasize the sound being taught in each lesson. For example, when you write and read *Act as an Animal* (page 9), emphasize the short *a* sound. Wherever possible, emphasize the sound being taught through repetitive use in your directions to students. It adds fun to the activity and gives students further experience hearing the sound in context.

- *Assess*—Use the Student Progress Chart reproducible (page 6) to track the phonemes students have mastered. Keep the charts on a clipboard by your desk. Update the charts as students work on the activities. When a student misses a lesson, photocopy and send home the activity page as homework. This involves parents and invites them to play a part in teaching their child to read.

Name _____

Student Progress Chart

Letters	Date Introduced	Date Reviewed	Date Mastered
Short Vowels			
a			
i			
o			
e			
u			
CVC words			
bat			
pin			
mop			
peg			
cup			
Long Vowels			
Two vowels together			
ee			
ai/ay			
ea			
oa			
ue			
Silent _e_			
a			
i			
o			
u			
Short words			
go, no, so			
he, be, she, we, me			
_R_-Controlled Vowels			
ar			
or			
er, ir, ur			

Phonics Without Worksheets: Vowels © 1999 Creative Teaching Press

Sight Word Activities

As your students progress, use the following activities to teach the sight words listed on page 8.

Sight Word Scramble

Write two or three sight words on the board. Distribute to each student an index card for every letter in each word. Have students write their name on one side of each card. Then, have students copy each letter of the sight words on the other side of their cards. Then, have students arrange their cards on their desk to form the words. Check student work for correct spelling and completeness, and read the words together as a class. Then, invite students to shuffle their cards and hide them facedown throughout the class. Have students go to a common location. On your signal, invite students to scramble through the classroom and collect cards (not their own) to spell out the sight words. Have students who have found all the cards sit in their seat. When all the cards have been located, read the words aloud together again. Collect all the cards and return them to their original owner at the end of the day for students to take home to read to parents.

Speed Reader Boxes

Before the lesson, cut 3" (7.6 cm) slits in the short sides of empty tissue boxes horizontal to the top and bottom and close to the "window" side of the box. Write on the board 10–20 sight words. Read each word to students, and remind them that these words do not follow phonetic rules. Divide the class into groups of three, and give each group a tissue box and two to five sentence strips or a long strip of adding machine tape. Invite students to copy the words on the sentence strips or adding machine tape, leaving at least two finger widths between words. Encourage students to thread each sentence strip or the adding machine tape through the slits so that only one word shows through the top of the box at a time. Students can take turns holding the box, pulling the strip slowly through the slits, and reading the words through the box top as they go by. Collect the finished "speed reader boxes," and keep them at a center where students may practice their sight word recognition.

Sight Word Stickers

Distribute ten labels to each student. Write 15–20 sight words on the board. Read the sight words aloud with students. Invite students to choose ten words to write on their labels. Encourage students to decorate their labels. Then, distribute lined paper to each student. Ask students to write several sentences, using one to three sight words in each sentence, and place a label on the line where each sight word should go.

Sight Words

a	do	live	some	was
all	find	many	the	were
are	from	most	their	what
as	has	of	there	who
been	have	on	they	world
by	his	one	to	would
come	into	other	too	you
could	is	said	two	your

Phonics Without Worksheets: Vowels © 1999 Creative Teaching Press

Act as an Animal

Short *a*

 Materials

✔ chart paper

✔ colored markers

✔ scissors

✔ sentence strips

 Preparation

Write *Act as an Animal* as a title on a large piece of chart paper. Make the *a* in each word a contrasting color. Cut sentence strips into cards, and write a short *a* word (see page 37 for ideas) on each card. Make a few additional cards with words that do not include the short *a* sound.

Display the chart paper, read the title aloud, and explain to students that the *a* in *act, as, an,* and *animal* is the short *a* sound. Invite students to brainstorm animal names that begin with short *a*, such as *antelope, anteater,* and *alligator,* and write their suggestions on the chart paper. Invite students to stand, and tell them that when they hear or see a word that has the short *a* sound they are to act like an animal until you turn the card over. Display a short *a* word card, and read it aloud. After a few seconds, place the card face-down on a desk. Discuss any long *a* words, such as *ape,* that may trick students into acting as an animal by simply saying *Listen again. The* a *does not make the short* a *sound in this word.* After all the cards have been read, display the animal list on a bulletin board and post the short *a* cards around it.

A as in Apple

Short *a*

 Materials

✔ red powdered drink mix in small paper cups

✔ apple for every 2 students

✔ cutting knife and cutting board

✔ sturdy toothpicks

 Preparation

Divide red powdered drink mix into small paper cups. Just before the activity, have a parent volunteer slice apples from top to bottom, avoiding the core so that each student will get almost half an apple with a clean, smooth inner surface. This will be the surface students etch in.

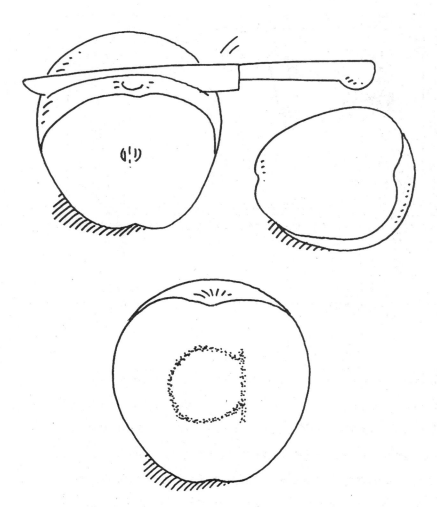

Draw on the board an apple tree. Have students brainstorm short *a* words, and write each correct word on an apple of the tree. Distribute to each student an apple half, a toothpick, and a cup of powdered drink mix. Model the activity once before inviting students to begin. Use a toothpick to carve an *a* into an apple. Then, dip the toothpick into the powdered mix, and dab it onto the *a* until there is a red *a* in the apple. When students have completed their apple, invite them to show you their apple *a* and then eat it.

Phonics Without Worksheets: Vowels © 1999 Creative Teaching Press

If It Is

Short *i*

Materials

✔ colored markers

✔ 2 sentence strips

✔ large bag of small household objects (measuring cup, hairbrush, sock, plastic flower, stuffed animal, etc.)

Preparation

Use a marker to write *If it is* _____, on a sentence strip. On a second sentence strip write *it is in* _____. Write the letter *i* of each word in a contrasting color. Collect a large bag of small household objects. Provide one object for each student.

Display the sentence strips on the board. Read the sentence strips aloud to students, and explain that the *i* in *if, it, is,* and *in* is the short *i* sound. Choose an item from the bag, and invite students to brainstorm where in the home that item is typically found. Model using the name of that object and where it is found to complete the sentence-strip sentence. For example, a hairbrush is often found in a bathroom, so the sentence can be completed by saying *If it is a hairbrush, it is in a bathroom.* Have students read each sentence strip and fill in the name of the object and where it is found in a home. Students can take turns pulling an object out of the bag and making their own sentence. To extend learning, invite each student to touch the corresponding words as he or she reads the sentence aloud.

Icky Insects

Short *i*

Materials

✔ tubes of frosting

✔ waxed paper

✔ book on insects

✔ chocolate creme-filled cookies, 2 or 3 for each student

✔ thin licorice of any color, 6–9" (15–23 cm) long, for each student

✔ large bag of miniature marshmallows

✔ small bag of miniature chocolate chips

✔ paper

Preparation

Use the directions at right to make an "icky insect" to use as an example. Squeeze a small amount of frosting onto a square of waxed paper for each student.

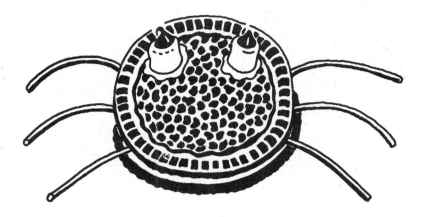

Read aloud a book about insects. Ask students which they think are icky and which are incredible insects. Tell students that some insects are helpful, such as bees that make honey and dragonflies that eat mosquitoes. Then, give each student a cookie, licorice, and a square of waxed paper with frosting. Have students gently twist the top off their cookie and break the licorice apart into pieces of equal lengths for "legs." Show students how to place the ends of the legs in the creme and place the top back on the cookie. Have students use their frosting to stick marshmallows on top of their cookie for "eyes." Show students how to top each marshmallow with frosting and miniature chocolate chips for "eyeballs." Distribute paper to each student, and write the following sentence frames on the board. Have students copy and complete the sentences to describe their imaginary insect.

My insect is _____.

It has _____.

It lives in _____.

Its name is _____.

Phonics Without Worksheets: Vowels © 1999 Creative Teaching Press

On/Off

Short o

Display the short o index cards in a pocket chart, and read aloud each card to students. Invite volunteers to point to the short o in words of their choice. Then, write on and off on the board, and read the words aloud. Explain that the os in on and off make the short o sound. Give each student two small index cards. Have each student copy the words on separate index cards. Then, have students read their cards aloud to a partner. When every student has done so successfully, explain to students that the game of "On/Off" is Simon Says with a twist. Choose a student to be Simon. Give him or her all the large index cards. Have Simon tell the class what to do with each card. For example, he or she may say to students *Simon says put* off *on your head.* Simon always says *Simon says* in front of his or her command. Have Simon display an index card. Tell students that if the index card has a short o word, they follow the directions Simon tells them to do. However, if the index card does not have a short o word, students do not follow the command. Set a time limit, at which time the old Simon picks a new student to be Simon.

Materials

✔ large and small index cards
✔ pocket chart

Preparation

Write 15–25 short o words on large index cards. Prepare an additional 5–10 large index cards with words without a short o.

Oliver the Octopus

Short o

Phonics Without Worksheets: Vowels © 1999 Creative Teaching Press

Materials

✔ short o picture cards (page 69)

✔ flavored gelatin mix

✔ hot plate, large bowls, and spoons

✔ water

✔ nonstick cupcake tins and 11 oz. (312 g) package of gummy worms

✔ scissors

✔ crayons or markers

✔ envelopes

✔ small paper plates and napkins

✔ construction or drawing paper

✔ glue

Preparation

Make Oliver the Octopus in advance by mixing flavored gelatin as described on the box. Follow the directions for molded gelatin, and pour mix into nonstick cupcake tins. (Tip: If you have enough tins, pour gelatin mix into every other row so Oliver's "legs" do not stick together.) Set the tins at a table, and have an adult volunteer supervise small groups of students in placing one end of eight gummy worms in each cup. When all the worms have been placed in the gelatin, move it to the refrigerator to harden completely. (This will take at least four hours.)

Distribute a page of short o picture cards to each student. Invite volunteers to say the name of each picture. Explain to students that the names of the items on the cards all contain the short o sound. When all of the cards have been read, encourage students to cut apart and color their cards. Have each student store his or her cards in an envelope labeled *short o*. When the gelatin has hardened, distribute small paper plates and napkins, and give each child an "octopus." (Wash your hands and loosen the worms that may be stuck together.) While students are devouring their octopus, distribute a large sheet of construction or drawing paper to each student. Have students use crayons or markers to draw their octopus and label their drawing *Oliver the Octopus*. Then, have them choose four to six short o picture cards to glue beneath Oliver the Octopus.

Fetch the Bell

Short *e*

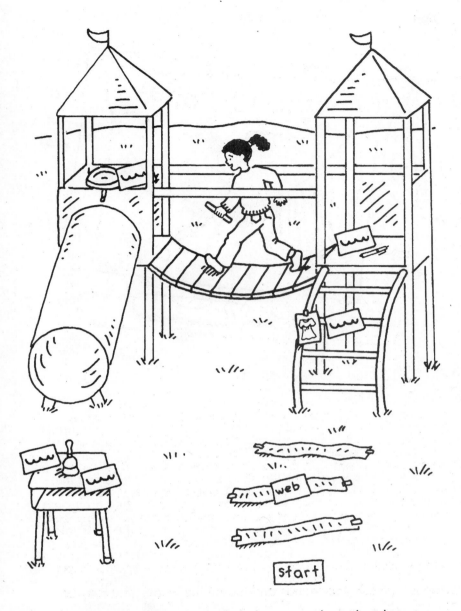

Phonics Without Worksheets: Vowels © 1999 Creative Teaching Press

Materials

✔ sentence strips

✔ scissors

✔ 2 cardboard tubes

✔ items with the short *e* sound in their name (e.g., *pen, helmet, desk, dress,* and *bed*) or illustrations of them

✔ 2 bells

✔ stopwatch

Preparation

Use playground equipment to create two obstacle courses. Write two lists of short *e* items such as *pen, helmet, desk, dress,* and *bed* on sentence strips, and cut the strips into individual word cards. Write *yes* on two cardboard tubes. Place short *e* items (or illustrations of them) and their corresponding titles throughout the courses. Place a bell at one end of each obstacle course, and make the other end the start and finish line.

Read aloud the word cards, and explain to students that the *e* in these words is the short *e* sound. Divide the class into two teams, and explain that the obstacle course will help them practice the short *e* sound. Have a volunteer help you demonstrate the path of the course. The first student in each line holds up the *yes* "baton" (cardboard tube), and reads it loudly. He or she then runs through the course, reading the names of the short *e* objects throughout the course, rings the bell, and returns to hand the baton to the next student at the starting point as quickly as possible. Time the teams, and challenge them to better their time.

My Alphabet Necklace

Short e

 Materials

✔ newspaper

✔ alphabet cereal

✔ colored cereal Os

✔ large and small bowl for
   each small group

✔ construction paper

✔ glue

✔ colored markers

 Preparation

Cover work areas with newspaper.
For each small group, pour alphabet
cereal into a large bowl and
colored cereal Os into a small
bowl.

Write 10–15 short e words on the board (see page 37 for ideas).
Read aloud the list, or invite student volunteers to decode the words.
Invite the class to say the short e sound together. Write *My Alphabet
Necklace* on the board, and read it aloud. Ask students to tell you
which of the three words has the short e sound in it. Underline the
e in *alphabet* and the first e in necklace. Tell students they are going
to make their own "alphabet necklace" today. Divide the class into
small groups, and give each group a bowl of alphabet cereal and
colored cereal Os. Invite each student to take a small handful of
cereal and use the letters to spell out one or more of the words
written on the board. After each student has successfully spelled out
a short e word with the cereal, distribute construction paper and
glue to each student. Have students use markers to draw a long "U"
to make a necklace. Have students glue each letter of their short e
words beneath their necklace, separating each short e word with a
colored cereal O. Challenge students to make as many short e
words as they can before they run out of cereal es. Invite students to
eat the extra letters when they feel peckish.

Phonics Without Worksheets: Vowels © 1999 Creative Teaching Press

Up, Up with Cups

Short *u*

Materials

✔ index cards

✔ foam or paper cup for each student

✔ pens

Preparation

Write words on separate index cards, at least half of which are short *u* words (see page 37 for ideas).

Distribute a foam or paper cup to each student. Have students use a pen to write their name and *The cup is up* on their cup. Have them line up and put their cup on their head upside down. Display the word cards individually, and invite students to walk towards you with their cup on their head whenever they see a short *u* word. When you display a word that does not have the short *u* in it, have students freeze. Those students who move when they should freeze or who drop their cup must return to the starting point. The first student to reach you can display the cards for the next round.

Yummy Upside-Down Cake

Short *u*

Materials

✔ index cards

✔ tape

✔ ⅓ cup (83 ml) butter or margarine

✔ nonstick cake pan

✔ ⅔ cup (167 ml) firmly packed brown sugar

✔ can of sliced pineapples

✔ maraschino cherries

✔ yellow cake mix

✔ oven

✔ plates and forks

Preparation

Write the following short *u* words on index cards: *bus, cub, cut, fun, gum, jug, mud, nut, rub, rug, tub, up,* and *us.* Tape them upside down on the board. If you do not have access to an oven at school, make an upside-down cake at home. Melt ⅓ cup (83 ml) butter or margarine in a nonstick cake pan. Stir in ⅔ cup (167 ml) firmly packed brown sugar. Lay pineapple slices on top of the mixture, and place a cherry in the center of each pineapple slice. Prepare yellow cake mix as directed on the box. Pour the batter on top of the pineapple mixture. Bake as directed. Bring the cake to school to flip out of its pan during the activity.

Read aloud the index cards, and explain to students that the *u* in these words is the short *u* sound. Make the upside-down cake together. While it bakes and cools, have an upside-down party! Have volunteers pull an upside-down short *u* word from the board, turn it right side up, and try to read it. To extend learning, play musical chairs with short *u* words taped under the chairs. When the music stops, have students look under their chair and read the word. Give each student a slice of upside-down cake, and invite students to sit on the floor, facing their chair, and use their chair seat as a table. Consider an "upside-down day" in which you follow your class schedule in reverse.

Phonics Without Worksheets: Vowels © 1999 Creative Teaching Press

Wiggle Words
Short Vowel Stories

 Materials

✔ chart paper

 Preparation

Copy each of the stories on pages 20 and 21 on chart paper. Underline the three "wiggle" words in each story. These stories emphasize short-vowel sounds and unite actions with words.

Display one of the stories, and indicate the three underlined wiggle words. Have students stand up, and tell them the action for each word. For example, in the short *a* story the action for the word *Max* is for students to hold up their hands and curl their fingers into claws. Have students practice the actions for each word once. Read the story aloud. Encourage students to do the appropriate action at each underlined wiggle word. Go through the story slowly the first time and then faster each subsequent time. As an extension, invite students to stand up, clap, touch their nose, or roll their shoulders each time they hear the short-vowel sound for that story.

Short *a*

Wiggle Word	Action
Max	hold up hands and curl fingers to represent claws
bad	shake finger
sat	sit down

A cat named **Max** had a **bad, bad** habit. He **sat** on everything including a rabbit. **Max sat** on a hat and a bat and a crab. **Max** had a habit that made us all mad. Along came an elephant, an old acrobat. He did a leap and fell on **Max.** "Get off of me! Look where you **sat!**" Now **Max** was a flat, sad cat.

Short *i*

Wiggle Word	Action
spin	turn around one time
Jim	salute
win	jump up with hands in the air

There was a man whose name was **Jim.** He hated to lose, but loved to **win!** One day his friend, Bill, said to **Jim,** "I will race you. I will **win.** I will beat you in a **spin.**"

"Ah," said **Jim.** "A race of **spins?** It sounds like fun. I'm going to **win.**"

"Go!" said Bill. They started to **spin.** Bill got dizzy, and he fell down. On the ground, he wore a frown. Who had a big, happy grin? Our friend **Jim** who loved to **win!**

Short *o*

Wiggle Word	Action
frog	squat down
hop	hop one time
stop	hold out hand, palm forward like a traffic cop

There was a **frog** who liked to **hop** so much that he would never **stop.** The **frog** would **hop** all night and day until one day he **hopped** away. Where did our friend the **frog hop** to? He jumped into the pouch of a kangaroo! In the pouch the **frog** got a ride. So he saw the countryside. Now Mr. **Frog** no longer **hops.** But the kangaroo can never **stop.**

Phonics Without Worksheets: Vowels © 1999 Creative Teaching Press

Short *e*

Wiggle Word	Action
hen	tuck hand under underarms to represent wings
red	point to something red
ten	wiggle ten fingers

Ben put his **red** pet **hen** in the nest. Then Ben went to get a friend. The **hen** laid **ten** eggs in the nest. Ben came back with his friend. Look at the **ten** eggs from my **red hen!** But where is the **hen?** The **ten** eggs are getting cold in their nest! Here she comes, here comes the **red hen** to warm her **ten** eggs.

Short *u*

Wiggle Word	Action
bug	wave arms like dangling legs
run	run quickly in place for a count of three
rug	lie down

There was a **bug** who lived in a snug, fuzzy **rug.** He thought it was fun to **run.** Every day the **bug** would **run** on the **rug.** One day there was a **bug** race in the **rug.** It started with the rising sun. The sun came up, the **bugs** were off! Their friends all watched yelling, "**Run! Run! Run!**" Hurrah! When it was done, our friend had won!

Magnetic Letters
CV Blending

 Materials

✔ magnetic letters, especially vowels and *b, d, f, g, m, n, p, r,* and *t*

✔ plastic resealable bags

✔ cookie sheets

✔ chart paper

 Preparation

Sort magnetic letters into groups, and place each group in a plastic resealable bag. Be sure each group has a set of vowels and a collection of the most common consonants.

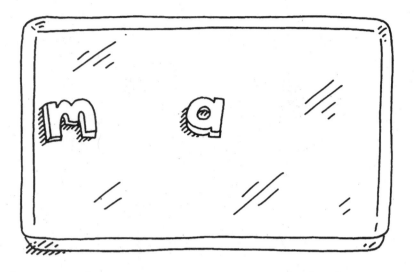

Review with the class the sounds of the short vowels before beginning the activity. Divide the class into groups of two to four students, and give each group a cookie sheet and a bag of magnetic letters. Model how to blend a consonant with a vowel by putting a magnetic *m* on one end of a cookie sheet and a magnetic *a* in the middle of the cookie sheet. Say /m/ while you push the letter *m* across the tray to meet up with the short *a*. Then, slide both letters across the length of the cookie sheet while saying *mmaaaa*. Have students tell you some words that start with the *ma* sound, such as *man, map* and *mad*. Repeat with *t* and *a*. Then, invite students to work in their small group to blend letter sounds with the magnetic letters. After students have had an opportunity to do the activity, invite them to tell you some of the words they formed and record these words on chart paper.

Arm in Arm
CV Blending

Phonics Without Worksheets: Vowels © 1999 Creative Teaching Press

Give each student a "letter necklace." Have students with consonants line up at one end of the room. Place the students with vowels in the middle of the room. Call out a consonant and a vowel, and have the consonant student make his or her sound until he or she meets up with the vowel student. (If there are more than one of the same vowel, have students take turns.) Have students link arms and walk together while saying their blended sound. When they reach the other end of the room, invite volunteers to think of words that begin with that sound.

Write common consonants (e.g., b, d, f, g, m, n, p, r, and t) and all the vowels on index cards. Shuffle the consonant cards, and invite the student to pick one. Choose a vowel card, and place it in the middle of the room. Invite the student to pick up the vowel card in the middle of the room and continue across the room while saying the blend aloud.

 Materials

✔ large index cards

✔ hole punch

✔ yarn

 Preparation

Write one letter on a large index card for every student in your class. Punch a hole in the top corners of each card, string yarn through the holes, and tie the ends together to make a necklace. Create cards for a variety of consonants and all the vowels. (In a class larger than 26, make additional vowel cards.)

Fast Track

CV Blending

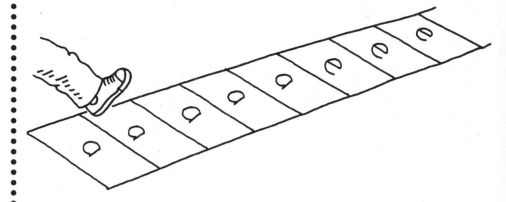

Materials

✔ index card for each student

✔ chalk if outdoors or one roll of clear shelf paper and a permanent marker if indoors

Preparation

Write each consonant on an index card, writing *qu* for *q*. If needed, make additional consonant cards so that every student has a card. On the playground, draw in chalk a train track like the illustration at right, or stick clear shelf paper to the floor if indoors and write the vowels (in the same pattern as the illustration) on the shelf paper with a permanent marker. Be sure to include sequentially five *as*, five *es*, two *is*, two *os*, and three *us* to accompany the pattern of the song at right.

Review short-vowel sounds with students. Then, teach them "I've Been Working on My Vowel Sounds," sung to the tune of "I've Been Working on the Railroad."

I've Been Working on My Vowel Sounds

I've been working on my vowel sounds all the live long day.

I've been working on my vowel sounds just to hear what sound they make.

Won't you come along and join me for a short vowel trip.

Won't you come along and join me while we hop and skip.

ba, ba, ba, ba, ba

be, be, be, be, be

bi, bi

bo, bo

bu, bu, bu

ba, ba, ba, ba, ba

be, be, be, be, be

bi, bi

bo, bo

bu

Show students the train track you have prepared. Give each student a consonant card, and line the class up at the short *a* end of the track. Invite students to pretend that the card in their hand is a ticket to ride on the track. Model taking a consonant "ticket," hopping down the track, and blending that consonant sound with each short vowel you land on. Encourage each student to take a "ride," hopping and blending down the track and chanting or singing "I've Been Working on My Vowel Sounds."

Phonics Without Worksheets: Vowels © 1999 Creative Teaching Press

Rhyme Time
CVC Words

Bat

Its face is like a pointy heart.

It likes to hide in caves so dark.

Is this a fox, a hill, or a cat?

Draw the wings of a friendly _____. (bat)

Bug

It has a little tiny head.

It is a creature that I dread.

Even with six legs for hugs,

I just don't like those creepy _____. (bugs)

Dog

This creature wants to be your friend;

Loyal and true until the end.

It's not a frog and not a hog.

It is, of course, a puppy _____. (dog)

 Materials

✔ chart paper

✔ white paper

✔ crayons or markers

 Preparation

Copy each rhyme at left onto chart paper.

Display one of the rhymes. Read aloud the rhyme, and have students suggest the missing word. Underline a CVC word in each rhyme, and explain the CVC pattern. Point out other words in the rhyme, and have students discuss whether or not they are CVC words. Then, give each student a sheet of white paper and crayons or markers. Invite students to draw a picture as you read the rhyme. Have students write the name of the animal they drew on their picture. Repeat with another rhyme, and collect the drawings to make individual books.

Word Lotto
CVC Words

 Materials

✔ short-vowel picture cards (pages 67–71) or a bag of miniature items

✔ CVC Lotto reproducible (page 27)

✔ scissors

 Preparation

Photocopy a set of short-vowel picture cards for each group in your class and four or five copies of the CVC Lotto reproducible. Cut and trim the cards. Write the name of each picture card in a space on the CVC Lotto reproducibles. Do not use a word more than once, and mix up the order on each of the reproducibles. Photocopy a set of the revised CVC Lotto reproducibles for each small group in your class. (Alternatively, collect from cake and party stores miniature items that have CVC names such as *pen, lid, pin, rock, stick, nut, bug, cap, top,* and *gum.* You will need one complete set for each group. Write the name of each object in a space on the CVC Lotto reproducibles.)

Divide the class into small groups of no more than five. Distribute to each group a set of the CVC Lotto reproducibles and a set of picture cards or miniatures. Invite students to say the names on the reproducible and match each picture card or miniature to the correct word. Encourage students to rotate places within a group and match new cards or items to words. Leave one set at a learning center for students to match in their free time. Consider placing a colored dot sticker on the back of each card and in the corner of the CVC Lotto reproducible to make the activity self-correcting.

Phonics Without Worksheets: Vowels © 1999 Creative Teaching Press

CVC Lotto

Touch and See
CVC Words

 Materials

✔ colored or glitter glue

✔ large index cards

✔ blank, unlined paper

✔ crayons

 Preparation

Use colored or glitter glue to write CVC words (see page 37 for ideas) with raised letters on large index cards (one word per card). Make sure your selection of words includes at least one representative of each vowel. Make at least one card for each student. Allow time for the glue to dry before beginning the activity.

Sit students in a circle, and have them close their eyes. Give each student a card, and let students feel their word with their fingers to try and guess what the word is. Then, invite students to open their eyes and check their word. Ask students to place their card in the middle of the circle in a pile. Shuffle the cards, and redistribute them so that students can play the game again with a new word. Extend the activity by distributing cards to students at their seats. Have students lay a piece of blank, unlined paper on top of their card. Encourage students to use the side of a crayon from which all the paper has been removed to rub over their paper. Invite students to trade cards and make new rubbings. Encourage students to take their rubbings home to read to parents.

Phonics Without Worksheets: Vowels © 1999 Creative Teaching Press

Poster Power
CVC Words

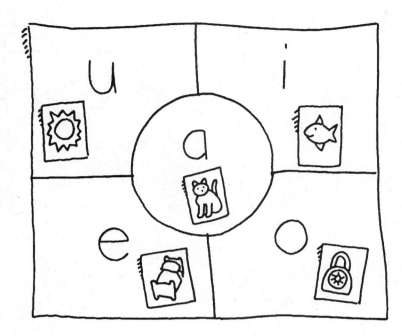

Phonics Without Worksheets: Vowels © 1999 Creative Teaching Press

 Materials

✔ chart or butcher paper for each group

✔ bag of miniature items or set of short-vowel picture cards (pages 67–71) for each group

 Preparation

For each small group, create a chart divided into five equal sections with a vowel written in the center of each section. Collect a bag of miniature items representing CVC words, or photocopy and cut apart a set of short-vowel picture cards for each group.

Divide the class into small groups. Distribute to each group a vowel chart and a bag of miniature items or picture cards. Invite the first student in each group to reach into the bag and pull out a miniature or picture card. Have the student say the name of the object and decide which short vowel is in the middle of the word. Then, have the student place the miniature or picture card on that vowel space of the chart and hand the bag to the next player. Continue the activity until the bag has been emptied. Invite students to help teammates who need assistance. Circulate and check completed charts.

 Set a timer for the student to try to improve his or her best time each time the game is played.

Lot-a-Dot
CVC Words

 Materials

- ✔ picture cards (pages 67–71) or miniature items representing CVC words (e.g., *pen, cup, block* and *lid*)
- ✔ scissors
- ✔ bag
- ✔ dot stickers
- ✔ paper
- ✔ 10 markers (e.g., pennies or pebbles) for each student
- ✔ crayons

 Preparation

Photocopy and cut apart the short-vowel picture cards, or gather a set of miniature items representing CVC words. Place the cards or items in a bag.

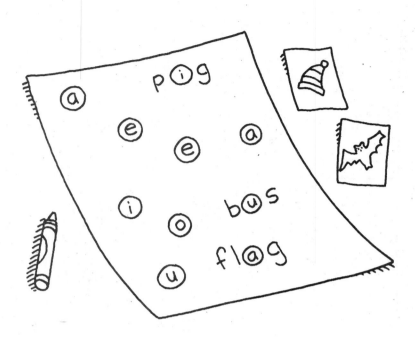

Distribute ten dot stickers, paper, and ten markers to each student. Ask students to put their dot stickers anywhere on their paper, but spaced well apart. Encourage students to use a crayon to write each vowel on a dot (being sure to write each vowel at least once). Circulate through the room, and give each student a turn to draw from the bag one item or card. Invite the student to say the word once, and then repeat it yourself, slowly emphasizing the vowel sound. Place the item or card back in the bag. Have all students look for the sticker that has the corresponding vowel on it and cover the dot with a marker. When they are done playing, have students clear the markers off their paper, and challenge them to write consonants before and after the vowels to spell words while you collect the markers.

Pick-Up Sticks
CVC Words

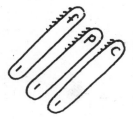 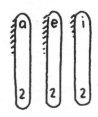 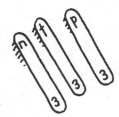

Divide the class into small groups, and give each group a foam top or bottom and a bundle of craft sticks. Ask each group to shuffle their craft sticks. Ask three students from each group to take turns selecting a stick to place into the appropriate slit to spell out a real CVC word. Then, have the groups take those three sticks out and lay them to the side. Challenge students to continue in this manner, taking turns at being the first, second, and third player, until they have formed as many real words as they can. When they have read their words to you, have groups shuffle their sticks and form additional words.

 Materials

✔ wide craft sticks
✔ colored markers
✔ rubber bands
✔ scissors
✔ foam container tops or bottoms

Preparation

Write a list on paper of 15–20 three-letter CVC words. For each word, write each letter at the top of a separate wide craft stick. Number or color-code the craft sticks to show the letter sequence. Make a set of six to ten words (three sticks each) for each small group of students, and bundle each set with a rubber band. Cut three slits in each foam container top or bottom (such as those used in restaurants) to hold the craft sticks, and number or color-code each one to match the craft sticks.

Rollin' Along

CVC Words

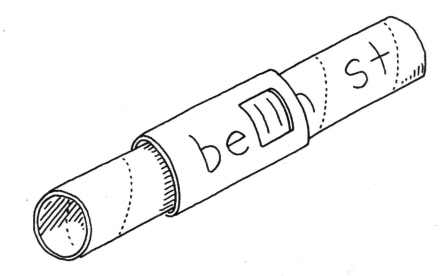

 Materials

✔ large collection of empty short and long cardboard tubes

✔ craft knife (teacher use only)

✔ paint and paintbrushes (optional)

 Preparation

Have students bring from home empty short and long cardboard tubes. (Consider asking a parent volunteer to do the following.) Fit the short tubes over the long tubes. If a short tube is too tight, cut a slit the length of the short tube so that it wraps around and easily slides the length of a large tube. Cut out a window in the right half of each short tube. To the left of the window, write a CV combination such as *sa, na,* or *be.* On the long tube, write endings such as *d, g, ll, n, t,* and *st.* Create a variety of CV combinations and endings so that each of the short vowels is represented and the tubes are not all the same (see page 37 and pages 67–71 for a list of possible words).

Distribute a set of tubes to each student. As students slide their small tube, invite them to read the CVC words formed (e.g., *bet, bed,* and *bell*). Encourage students to find a partner with a different consonant-vowel combination with whom to trade. Consider inviting students to paint their tubes with light colors before you write the CV combinations and endings. Store the tubes at a learning center so that students can use them over and over again.

Phonics Without Worksheets: Vowels © 1999 Creative Teaching Press

Ghost Words

CVC Words

Have students complete this activity on a sunny day. Invite students
to brainstorm CVC words, and record their suggestions on the
board or chart paper. Then, divide the class into pairs, and give
each pair a paintbrush and a cup of water. Take the class outside
to a concrete surface, and invite partners to take turns using their
paintbrush and water to write CVC words on the pavement. As one
partner writes words the other reads them before they disappear.
Have partners swap roles after each word.

 Materials

✔ cup of water and paintbrush for
   every 2 students

✔ chart paper (optional)

 Preparation

Fill with water enough cups for every
two students in your class.

Letter Twister
CVC Words

 Materials

✔ CVC Words reproducible (page 37)

✔ permanent marker

✔ plain, plastic tablecloth or an old, white sheet for each small group

 Preparation

Make a "twister" sheet for each group by using a permanent marker to print six rows of five letters on a tablecloth or an old, white sheet. Include two sets of vowels and a repetition of high-frequency consonants (e.g., *b, m, r,* and *s*) in random order. Then, photocopy the CVC Words reproducible for easy reference.

Divide the class into groups of four or five, and give each group a twister sheet. Choose a word from the CVC Words reproducible, and say it aloud. Encourage one student from each group to use his or her hands and feet to touch all the letters in the word. Then, invite the next student in each group to touch the letters of the next word. Students can touch the same letter, and a student who loses his or her balance can start over with the next word. Team members can help each other spell out the words if needed.

Hopscotch Spelling

CVC Words

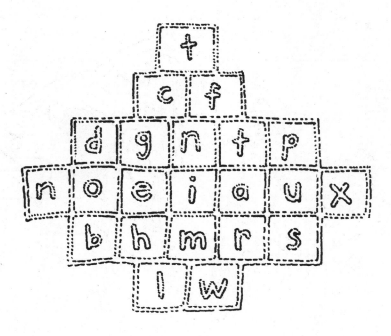

Take the class to a paved area of the school. Divide the class into two to four teams (as space allows). Draw in chalk a hopscotch pattern (as shown above) for each team. Choose a word from the CVC Words reproducible, and read it aloud. The first player from each team hops on the letters to spell the word, jumping from box to box. If players are correct, they write the word in chalk on the ground near their hopscotch pattern. If a player is incorrect, he or she does not record the word in chalk. Repeat the process with other players and CVC words until everyone has had at least two turns. The team that spells the most words correctly wins.

Materials

✔ CVC Words reproducible (page 37)

✔ chalk

Preparation

Photocopy the CVC Words reproducible for easy reference.

Help Tell a Story
CVC Words

 Materials

✔ *The Three Little Pigs* story

✔ chart paper

✔ small index cards

 Preparation

Write *pig, pigs, sticks, big, bad, let, in, not, fell, pot, hot,* and *end* on chart paper.

Display the chart paper, and read aloud the list of words. Then, give each student six small index cards. Have half the class copy the first six words on their small index cards and half the class copy the second six words on their small index cards. Read aloud *The Three Little Pigs.* Each time you read a word that also appears on an index card, have students hold up the corresponding card.

CVC Words

bag	bib	box	bed	bug
bat	big	dog	bell	bus
cat	bit	doll	hen	cup
hat	hip	fox	leg	hug
mad	pig	hog	men	mud
man	pin	hop	net	nut
map	sip	hot	red	rug
rat	six	log	tell	run
sad	wig	mop	web	sun

Phonics Without Worksheets: Vowels © 1999 Creative Teaching Press

Short and Long Game

Short- and Long-Vowel Discrimination

 Materials

✔ index cards
✔ pocket chart

Have students sit in a circle on the floor. Display each index card in a pocket chart. Review the short-vowel sound each letter makes. Then, tell students that sometimes these vowels make another sound in which they say their name. Tell students the long-vowel sound for each vowel, and tell them these sounds are called long-vowel sounds. After reviewing all the vowel sounds, invite students to play the "Short and Long Game." When you say a short-vowel sound, have students stay short, sitting on their heels and crouching. When you say a long-vowel sound, have students reach up to the ceiling, resting on their knees. Have students practice this skill as you point to individual vowels and say either their long or short sound. Then, recite the nursery rhymes (listed below), and ask students to reach up when they hear a long-vowel sound. (Note that students are sitting back on their heels during other parts of the rhyme.) Encourage students by nodding and pointing to the correct letter card that corresponds with each vowel sound.

 Preparation

Write each vowel on a separate index card.

Little Miss Muffet sat on her tuffet
Eating (UP) *her curds and whey* (UP);
Along came (UP) *a spider* (UP)
Who sat down beside (UP) *her*
And frightened (UP) *Miss Muffet away.* (UP)

Jack be (UP) *nimble. Jack be* (UP) *quick.*
Jack jump over (UP) *the candlestick.*

Continue the activity with other nursery rhymes, including "Mary Mary Quite Contrary," "Jack Sprat," "Peter, Peter Pumpkin Eater," and "There Was an Old Woman."

Phonics Without Worksheets: Vowels © 1999 Creative Teaching Press

Long and Short Steps

Short- and Long-Vowel Discrimination

 Materials

✔ 2 bags

✔ miniature toys or picture cards (pages 67–78) representing words with long- and short-vowel sounds

 Preparation

Fill two bags with miniature toys or picture cards representing words with long- and short-vowel sounds. Provide at least ten items in each bag.

Divide the class in half, and then divide each team in half again. Have the two halves of each team line up against opposite sides of the room. Review short- and long-vowel sounds, and tell students they will play a game to practice hearing long and short vowels. Give the first student on each team a bag of picture cards or items, and invite the players to reach in their bag for one card or item and say its name. Ask students to take a short step when they hear a short vowel and a long step when they hear a long vowel. After they have taken their long or short step, have them choose another item. They will continue in this manner until they reach the other side and then give their bag to the first student in line and go to the end of that line. The game is over when one team has all of its players back in their original location.

 Invite the student to race you across the room, taking short steps with short vowels and long steps with long vowels.

ee **Tree**

Two Vowels Together

Materials

✔ *ee* Leaves reproducible (page 41)

✔ multilimbed tree branch, rocks or sand, and a bucket or coffee can

✔ large index card

✔ green construction paper or card stock

✔ chart paper

✔ scissors

✔ hole punches

✔ twist ties from plastic bags

Preparation

Place a multilimbed tree branch in a bucket or coffee can of rocks or sand. Write *ee Tree* on a large index card, and prop the card against the base of the branch. Photocopy on green construction paper or card stock a class set of the *ee* Leaves reproducible.

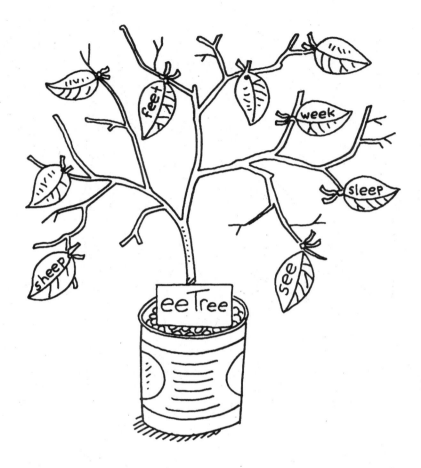

Tell students that the short *e* turns into a long *e* when there are two *e*s together. Write *tree* on the board. Tell students that two *e*s together make the long *e* sound. Encourage students to brainstorm *ee* words. Record their suggestions on chart paper. Model cutting a leaf from the *ee* Leaves reproducible and writing an *ee* word from the chart paper on it. Punch a hole in the leaf, and attach it to the branch with a twist tie. Give each student an *ee* Leaves reproducible, and invite students to cut out leaves and write *ee* words on them. Encourage students to fill the *ee* tree with *ee* leaves.

Possible *ee* words include the following:

bee	eel	keep	sheep	three
beep	feed	need	sleep	weed
bleed	feel	peek	speed	week
cheek	feet	peel	street	
creek	free	queen	sweep	
deep	green	see	sweet	

Phonics Without Worksheets: Vowels © 1999 Creative Teaching Press

ee **Leaves**

Walking Together

Two Vowels Together

 Materials

✔ large index cards

✔ 2 hula hoops or masking tape

✔ pocket chart

✔ masking tape

✔ lined writing paper

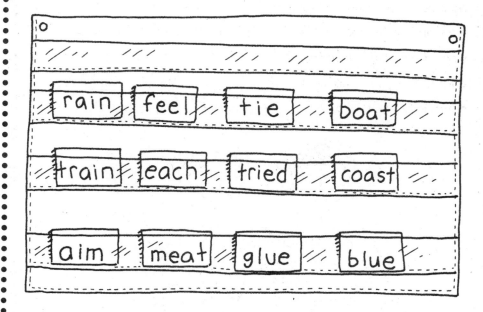

 Preparation

Make one letter card each of *a, i, o, u,* and two cards of *e.* Place two hula hoops side by side on the floor or use masking tape to make two circles. Copy 15–20 vowel-pair words (see list on page 43) onto large index cards, and display them in a pocket chart.

Display the pocket chart of vowel-pair words. Tell students that sometimes when two vowels get together, the first one says its letter. Read with students the words with vowel pairs. Have volunteers locate vowel pairs that make the long *a, i, o, e,* and *u* sounds. Then, choose six students to be the vowels, and tape a letter card to each student's shirt. Have the vowel students stand near the hula hoops or taped circles at the front of the classroom. Distribute lined writing paper to each student. Sit in front of the vowel students with your back to the rest of the class. Hold up a vowel-pair card, and call out the word. (The vowel students will see the word on the card, and all students will hear you read it.) Encourage students who wear the vowels in the word to jump into a hoop, with the first vowel being on their right, your left, so that the students in the audience read them in the correct order. Then, invite the two vowels to hook arms and walk together around the room while the student representing the first vowel says its name.

Phonics Without Worksheets: Vowels © 1999 Creative Teaching Press

For example, when you call out the word *dream*, *e* jumps into the
right hula hoop and *a* jumps into the left one. *E* and *a* hook arms and
walk around the room while *e* says his or her sound. Have the class
write *dream* on their paper. When all the vowel students have had
a turn, have them choose new students to take their place and then
return to their seats to write the next word. Check spelling as a class.

Possible vowel-pair words include the following:

aim	clue	faith	leash	meat	stream
bean	coast	feel	load	rain	tie
blue	dear	flies	loan	road	train
boat	each	glue	mail	soap	tried

*Lay a board at an angle against a chair to make a
ramp. Attach vowel index cards with putty or dough to
the tops of toy cars. After you have read a word from
your list, invite the student to slide the cars side by side
down the ramp while saying the first vowel's name.
Then, encourage the student to write the word on paper.*

Sneak a Peek

Two Vowels Together

Materials

✔ chart paper

✔ 8½" x 11" (21.6 cm x 28 cm) paper

✔ scissors

✔ pencil, crayon, or marker

Preparation

Copy 15–20 vowel-pair words on chart paper. Cut 8½" x 11" (21.6 cm x 28 cm) paper into 8½" x 8½" (21.6 cm x 21.6 cm) squares.

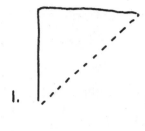
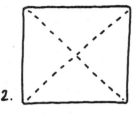
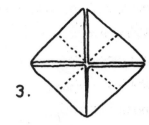
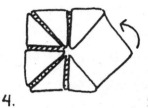
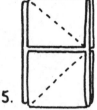

Display the chart paper with vowel pairs. (Note: Words with *ay* are included in this category.) Have students read the list with you. Invite volunteers to locate vowel pairs that make the long *a, i, o, e,* and *u* sounds and underline the vowel pairs. Distribute the paper squares, and model how to make a "Sneak a Peek" fortune-teller as students follow along.

1. Fold the square diagonally in half to make a triangle.

2. Open the paper and fold again in the other direction.

3. Open the paper again and fold all four corners into the middle.

4. Flip the square over and fold all four corners into the middle again.

5. Fold in half toward the inside. Then open and crease the other half.

6. Stick a thumb and forefinger under the flaps.

7. Open and close toward the center.

Phonics Without Worksheets: Vowels © 1999 Creative Teaching Press

When students have finished making their Sneak a Peek, have them label the four outside diamonds with this chant:

When two vowels
get together
the first one
names its letter

On the inner triangles, have students use a pencil, crayon, or marker to write vowel pairs such as *ai, ay, ea, ee, oa,* and *ue.* Next, direct students to lift the flaps and write three words containing the vowel combinations. When the Sneak a Peeks are completed, invite students to form pairs. Encourage the first partner to move his or her Sneak a Peek by pressing one finger and thumb of each hand together and then pressing fingers and thumbs of both hands apart, as he or she says the chant. The other partner picks a flap and guesses a word that may be hiding under it, and then they trade places.

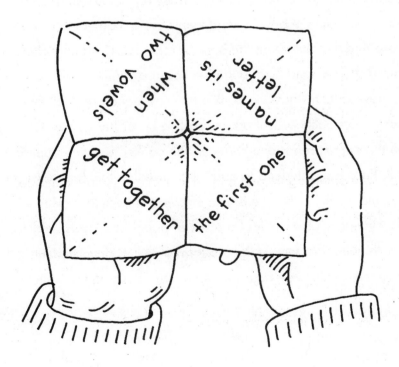

Play Pay Day

Two Vowels Together

Phonics Without Worksheets: Vowels © 1999 Creative Teaching Press

Materials

✔ *Ay Money* reproducible (page 47)

✔ scissors

✔ markers

✔ paper

Preparation

Photocopy a class set of the *Ay Money* reproducible.

Have students brainstorm *ay* words, and write their suggestions on the board. Give each student an *Ay Money* reproducible, and ask students to cut out the bills. Have students use a marker to write one *ay* word and their name on the back of each bill. Divide the class into small groups, and have students choose a "banker" at each table. Have students give the banker their *ay* money, and tell the banker to give each student a turn reading his or her *ay* words. When the student reads one correctly, the banker pays the student the bill. Encourage students to earn all their bills back, and have students switch roles so that the bankers have a chance to read their words. Have each student fold a piece of paper into thirds, folding the last third over to form a flap, to form a wallet. Have students write on their wallet *Pay Day* and store their money in the wallet.

Possible *ay* words include the following:

away	gray	may	pray	stay
bay	hay	maybe	ray	stray
clay	jay	pay	say	sway
day	lay	play	spray	tray

Ay Money

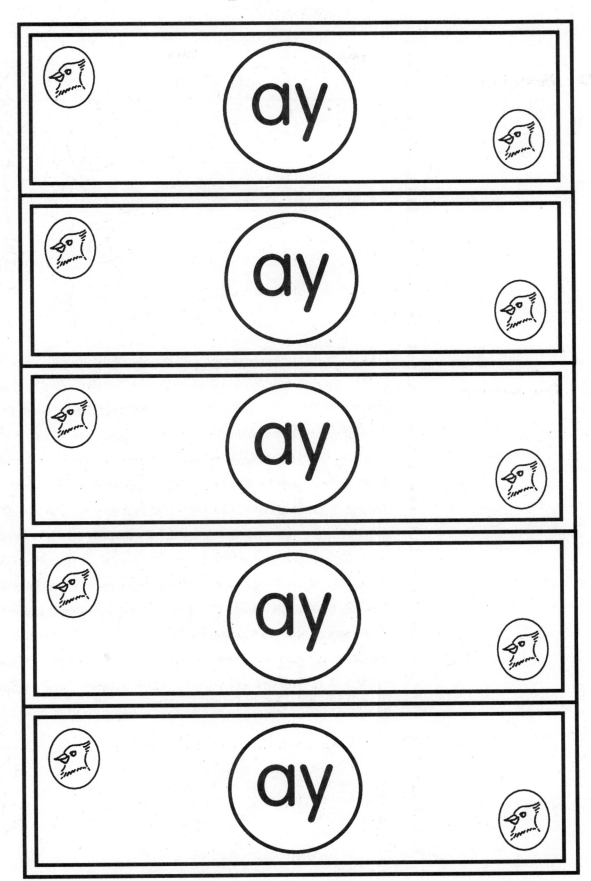

Super *E* Strips

Silent *e*

Phonics Without Worksheets: Vowels © 1999 Creative Teaching Press

Materials

✔ class set of "Super Silent *e*" poem

✔ chart paper

✔ paper strips

✔ envelopes

✔ glue

Preparation

Photocopy the "Super Silent *e*" poem. Write at least ten of the CVC and silent *e* word pairs (at right) on chart paper or the board (see page 49 for ideas). Cut paper into 1" x 4" (2.5 cm x 10 cm) strips.

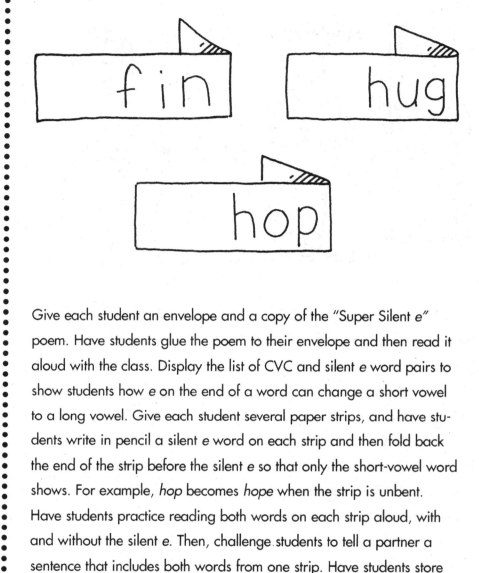

Give each student an envelope and a copy of the "Super Silent *e*" poem. Have students glue the poem to their envelope and then read it aloud with the class. Display the list of CVC and silent *e* word pairs to show students how *e* on the end of a word can change a short vowel to a long vowel. Give each student several paper strips, and have students write in pencil a silent *e* word on each strip and then fold back the end of the strip before the silent *e* so that only the short-vowel word shows. For example, *hop* becomes *hope* when the strip is unbent. Have students practice reading both words on each strip aloud, with and without the silent *e*. Then, challenge students to tell a partner a sentence that includes both words from one strip. Have students store their silent *e* strips in their envelope.

Super Silent e

Super *e* is super neat.
He can change a *pet* to *Pete*,
bit to *bite*,
my, oh my,
rob to *robe*,
way to go,
tub to *tube*,
yes, it's true,
can to *cane*,
that's the way
super silent *e*.

Super *E* Seat

Silent *e*

 Materials

✔ large index cards

Select one student to be the first "Super *e*" and give him or her the bold *e* card. Randomly distribute the remaining cards to other students. Place four chairs in a row facing the class. Choose a three-letter word from the list below. Invite students who hold the corresponding letter cards to sit in the first three chairs in correct letter sequence, and then with a great deal of production, invite Super *e* to "transform" the short-vowel word into a long-vowel word. Emphasize that Super *e* changes the word without making a sound of its own. Have students return to their seats, and choose a new short-vowel word to continue the activity. Invite students who do not have an index card to take turns being silent *e*.

 Preparation

Write on separate large index cards all the letters of the alphabet except *j, q, x, y,* and *z*. Make the letter *e* card extra bold.

can	cane	bid	bide	lob	lobe
cap	cape	bit	bite	mop	mope
fad	fade	fin	fine	nod	node
fat	fate	kit	kite	not	note
gal	gale	pin	pine	rob	robe
mad	made	rip	ripe	tot	tote
man	mane	sir	sire	cub	cube
mat	mate	cop	cope	cut	cute
nap	nape	dot	dote	dud	dude
tap	tape	hop	hope	tub	tube

 Have the student lay the first three letter cards of a word in a row on the floor. Invite him or her to wear a cape (towel) with an e pinned on to be Super e and form the long-vowel word.

Go Fish

Short Words

✔ 8 small index cards for each student

✔ colored markers

 Preparation

Write *go, so, no, he, be, she, we, me,* and *hi* on the board, and read the words aloud. Explain to students that short (one-syllable) words that end in a vowel usually have the long-vowel sound. Give each student eight small index cards. Have students use a colored marker to write each word on a separate index card to make a full set. (Students who finish quickly can make an extra set.) Divide the class into groups of two to four to play this version of Go Fish. Tell students the object of the game is to make pairs and be the first to run out of cards. Ask each group of players to combine their cards together to make one deck of cards. Have one student shuffle the cards and deal five cards to each player. Invite students to try to form pairs from the cards in their hand and place pairs on the table. Invite the first student to look at his or her hand and choose a card to try to match. For example, a student with the *so* card asks another student in the group *Do you have any so*s *in your hand?* If he or she has the card, it is given to the student asking for it. If not, the player asking has to *go fish* by drawing the top card off the remaining pile. Play continues until all of the cards have been matched.

Shopping Cart

R-Controlled Vowels: ar

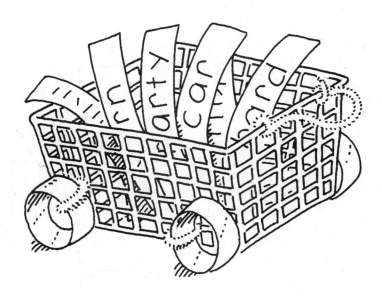

Materials

✔ mushroom or strawberry baskets
✔ small cardboard tubes
✔ pipe cleaners
✔ index cards
✔ scissors

Preparation

Wash and dry mushroom or strawberry baskets as needed.

Give each student a basket, a small cardboard tube, three pipe cleaners, and three to four index cards. Have students cut their tube into fourths to resemble wheels. Have students cut two pipe cleaners in half and then use the four halves to attach the wheels to their basket. Then, ask students to wrap their last pipe cleaner around the front edge of their basket to look like a handle. Invite students to pretend they are going shopping for *ar* words. Have them brainstorm *ar* words while you write their suggestions on the board. When students have brainstormed 20–25 words, have them cut their index cards in fourths and then copy 12–16 *ar* words onto the small cards. Divide the class into pairs, and have students compare their *ar* words by reading each card to their partner.

Possible *ar* words include the following:

arm	dark	harp	part	star
art	dart	jar	party	start
bark	far	large	scar	tar
barn	farm	lark	scarf	target
car	fart	march	shark	yard
card	garden	mark	sharp	yarn
cart	hard	Mars	smart	
chart	harm	park	spark	

Fort

R-Controlled Vowels: or

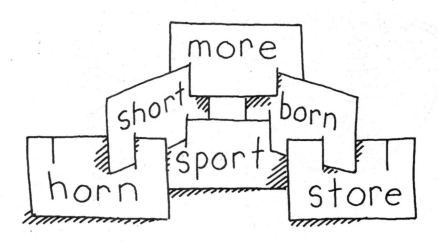

Have students brainstorm words with *or,* and write their suggestions on the board. Then, give each student ten small index cards. Have students use a marker to write an *or* word on each card. Ask students to use scissors to make two 1" (2.5 cm) cuts on one of the long sides of each card. Divide the class into teams, or invite students to choose a partner. Encourage pairs to work together to build an *or* "fort" by interlocking the cards at their cuts. Challenge students to build a high fort and then read all the *or* words on their fort before it falls. For an *or* snack, you can invite each student to read several words off the board and reward students with an Oreo.

Possible *or* words include the following:

before	fork	north	short	stork
born	form	orbit	sore	storm
cord	fort	order	sort	thorn
corn	horn	pork	sport	torch
for	more	report	store	torn

 Materials

✔ 10 small index cards for each student

✔ markers

✔ scissors

✔ Oreo® cookies (optional)

 Preparation

Phonics Without Worksheets: Vowels © 1999 Creative Teaching Press

Stir the Words

R-Controlled Vowels: *er, ir,* and *ur*

Materials

✔ white paper

✔ lined paper

✔ scissors

✔ large bowl

✔ spoon

Preparation

Have students brainstorm *er, ir,* and *ur* words, and write their suggestions on the board. Explain that *er, ir,* and *ur* all make the same sound. Group the words by their spelling. Give each student a piece of white paper and a piece of lined paper. Have students fold the white paper into eight sections, and then cut apart each section on the fold. Have students choose any eight words off the board and write them in pencil on the lined paper. Then, have students write each of the words on the lined paper on a separate piece of the eight small sections of paper. Have students place the small pieces of paper into a large bowl. Ask volunteers to take turns stirring the words, and then invite a student to select a paper from the bowl. He or she reads aloud the word. Point it out on the board. Encourage students to read the list on their paper and check it off or underline it if they have it. When everyone has had a turn stirring and/or picking out a word, ask students to count how many of their words are checked or underlined. To extend the learning, save the word scraps in the bowl and invite students to sort the words into *er, ir,* and *ur* piles. Read the words aloud, and have students tell you which pile they should go to.

Possible *er, ir,* and *ur* words include the following:

brother	mother	bird	girl	burn	purple
father	over	chirp	shirt	burst	purse
germ	sister	dirt	sir	curb	turn
her	thunder	first	swirl	fur	turtle

Super Butter Maker

R-Controlled Vowels: er, ir, and ur

Materials

- heavy whipping cream, 1 pint (500 ml) for every 10 students
- small plastic containers (such as film canisters)
- filled ice chest
- colored markers
- chart paper
- salt
- plastic knives
- bread

Preparation

Store whipping cream and plastic containers in an ice chest until you are ready to pour the cream. Use a marker to write the recipe (at right) on chart paper.

Tell students that they will become superb butter makers. Explain that *er, ir,* and *ur* make the same sounds. Read aloud the recipe, and invite students to take turns locating and tracing over the *er*s, *ir*s, and *ur*s in another color. Then, read the recipe again, inviting volunteers to read the *er, ir,* and *ur* words as you come to them. When this is completed, follow the recipe together. While students are shaking their cream into butter, have them brainstorm more *er, ir,* and *ur* words, and write their suggestions on the board.

Sup**er** Butt**er** Mak**er**s

1. F**ir**st wash yo**ur** hands to dist**ur**b the g**er**ms and d**ir**t.
2. Meas**ur**e 2 tablespoons (30 ml) cream into a cold contain**er**.
3. Th**ir**d, ret**ur**n the lid to the contain**er**.
4. Hold on f**ir**mly.
5. Sw**ir**l and wh**ir**l the butt**er**.
6. Shake it until yo**ur** hand looks like a bl**ur**.
7. If it gets warm, ret**ur**n the contain**er** to the cool**er** for a while.
8. Open the contain**er**. Is it butt**er**?
9. Drain out the wat**er**.
10. Ins**er**t a dash of salt. St**ir** it.
11. S**er**ve the sup**er**b snack. You des**er**ve it. You c**er**tainly w**er**e a sup**er** butt**er** mak**er**.

Phonics Without Worksheets: Vowels © 1999 Creative Teaching Press

Mini-Book Assembly

Photocopy and trim the mini-books (pages 58–63). Have students follow these steps to make each mini-book:

1. Fold the paper in half.

2. Cut along the dotted line halfway through the folded paper.

3. Hold the paper with the cut at the top. Fold the left flap forward and the right flap backward.

4. Keeping the flaps folded, open the paper so you can see the blank side.

5. Fold the paper in half so the pictures face outward.

6. Fold the paper in half again. Be sure page one is in front.

1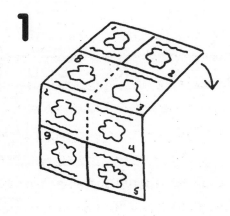

2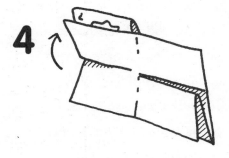

3

4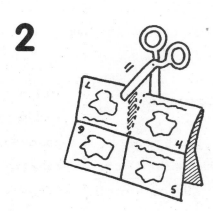

5

6

Mini-Book Activity Ideas

Enjoy these mini-book activities with your students:

- After reading a mini-book a few times with your class, photocopy and cut into individual pages enough copies of the book to give a page to each student. Have students locate and underline the repeated vowel sounds on their page. Invite students to think of two new words that have that same vowel sound and tell them to a neighbor.

- Photocopy a class set of the mini-book, and distribute one to each student. Model how to assemble the book, and invite students to do so. Read the mini-book with students, and then invite them to underline or highlight a specific vowel sound.

- Copy the text of each page of a mini-book on a separate sentence strip. Then, photocopy the picture cards for the corresponding vowel sounds, cut them apart, and glue them to index cards. Display each sentence strip, and invite students to read it aloud. Next, choose several volunteers, give each one a picture card, and have them say the name of their picture card. Have students match their picture card with a word on a sentence strip that has that vowel sound. Display each picture card above or below the word with the same vowel sound.

• Photocopy and cut into individual pages enough copies of the book to give a page to each student. As you read each page, have students identify the repeating vowel sound. For each of the vowel sounds repeated in the book, ask those students who have that vowel sound in many of the words on their page to underline or highlight it. After all students have located their repeating vowel sounds, give each student an index card on which to copy the words that begin with that vowel sound. Tape four large squares of shelf paper, sticky side out, onto a wall. Stick a letter card representing each vowel sound to the top of each shelf-paper square. Ask students to stick their index card to the square that has their vowel sound on it.

• Photocopy the mini-book to an overhead transparency, and cut it into individual frames. Display two pages at a time, matching the repeated vowel sounds. Have students sit in a circle, and have a large ball of yarn ready. Read aloud the first two pages, and invite students to identify the repeated vowel sound. Then, challenge them to think of other words that have the same vowel sound. Have each student share his or her contribution. As students are sharing, roll the ball of yarn over to them. As more words are generated, the "web" of yarn grows. Continue until all vowel sounds in the mini-book are reviewed, and take a photo of the completed web.

Mini-Book One
Short *a*, Short *i*

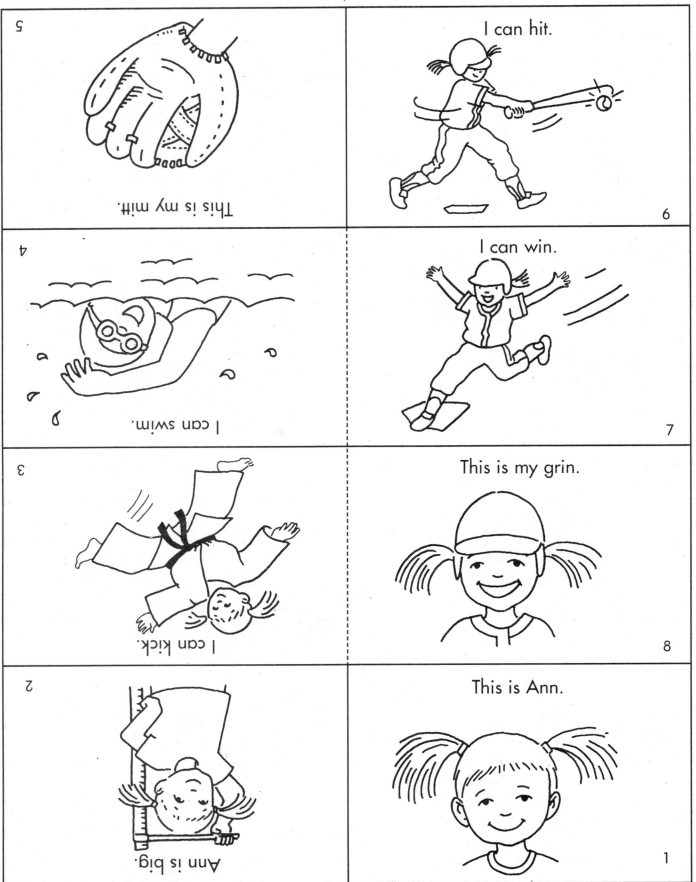

5

This is my mitt.

I can hit.

6

4

I can swim.

I can win.

7

3

I can kick.

This is my grin.

8

2

Ann is big.

This is Ann.

1

Mini-Book Two
Short e, Short o, Short u

Uh, oh. The pop drops.

6

5

Uh, up went the pop.

Yuck, Ed.

7

4

Ed will not stop.

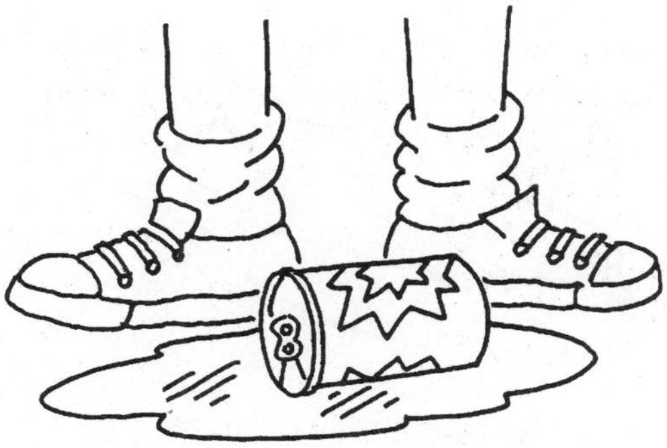

Messy, wet, fizzy pop.

8

3

Stop, Ed, stop.

Ed likes pop.

1

2

Ed jumps up. Ed hops.

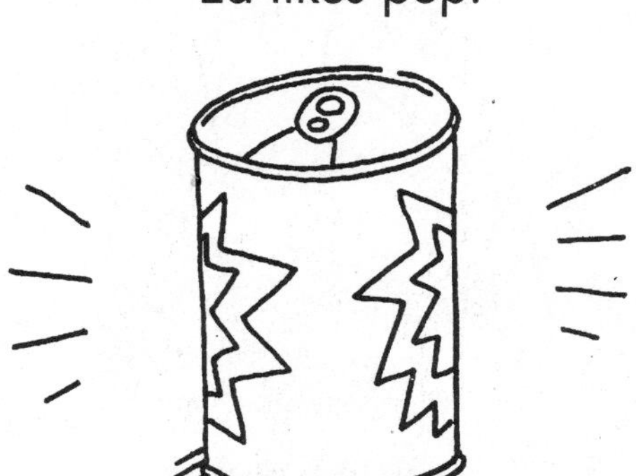

Phonics Without Worksheets: Vowels © 1999 Creative Teaching Press

Mini-Book Three

Short *a, i, o, e, u*

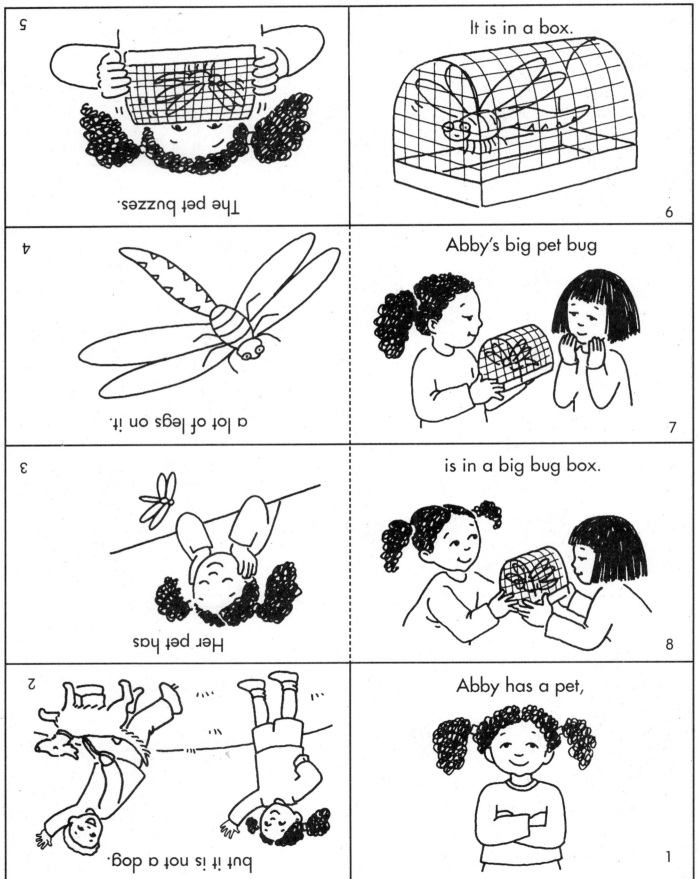

5

The pet buzzes.

It is in a box.

6

4

a lot of legs on it.

Abby's big pet bug

7

3

Her pet has

is in a big bug box.

8

2

but it is not a dog.

Abby has a pet,

1

Mini-Book Four
Two Vowels Together

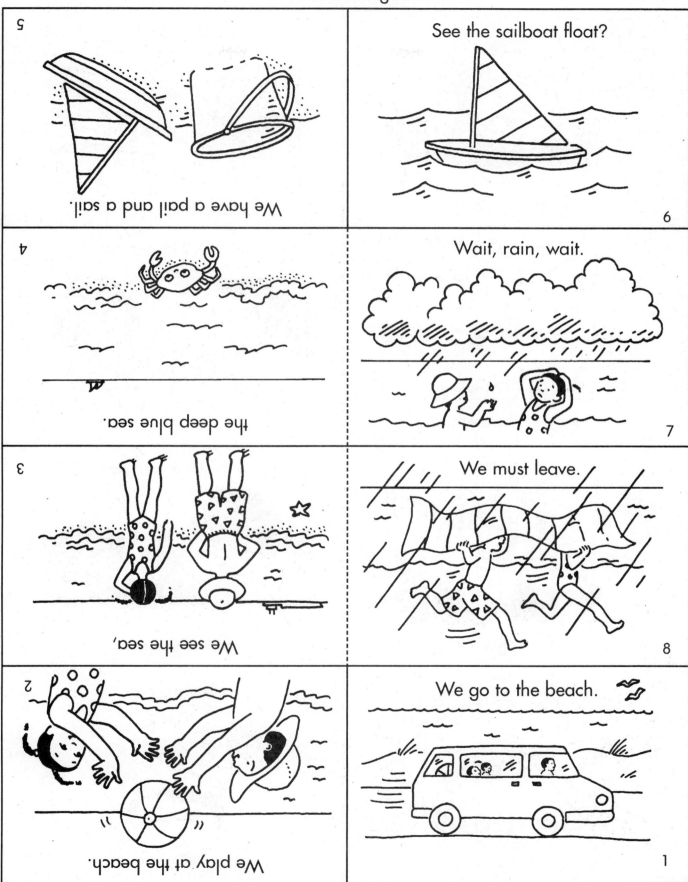

See the sailboat float?

6

We have a pail and a sail.

5

Wait, rain, wait.

7

the deep blue sea.

4

We must leave.

8

We see the sea,

3

We go to the beach.

1

We play at the beach.

2

Mini-Book Five
Silent e

I like to ride my bike.

5

I like to fly my kite.

6

I play a tune in June.

4

I hope you like my note.

7

I like to play my flute.

3

It is just a silly joke.

8

Here, I made you a cake.

2

I like to bake.

1

Phonics Without Worksheets: Vowels © 1999 Creative Teaching Press

Mini-Book Six
Two Vowels and Silent e Review

5

for the pie you bake.

See my smile?

6

4

I would take a train

It is a mile wide.

7

3

I would ride down the road.

I ate the peach pie.

8

2

I would creep down a street.

I would wait and hope.

1

Picture- and Letter-Card Activities

Here are a few activities to get students started with the picture and letter cards (pages 67–80). Additional cards can be created by gluing pictures from magazines or catalogs to index cards. Laminate the cards or cover them with clear shelf paper for greater durability.

• Index Box—Obtain several index-card boxes that include alphabet tabs. Remove the consonant tabs. Mark the vowel tabs as long vowels, and use the back side of five tabs to make short-vowel tabs. Attach a small envelope to the back of each box. Photocopy picture cards to paper or card stock, and cut them apart. Make one set of cards for each box. Place the picture cards into the envelope. Have students take the picture cards from the envelope and file each one (by vowel sound) behind the corresponding letter tab.

• Memory—Photocopy and cut apart the picture and letter cards for the phonemes on which you want students to focus. Divide the class into small groups. Invite a student to shuffle the cards and lay them facedown on the table. Have students take turns picking up pairs and trying to match phonemes. Cards that do not match are placed

facedown again. The player with the most pairs at the end of the game gets to shuffle the cards and lay them down again to start a new game.

• Go Fish—Photocopy and cut apart the picture and letter cards for the vowels on which you want students to focus. Consider adding additional picture cards. Make a set for each small group of two to four students. Divide the class into groups of two to four students, and give each group a set of cards. Tell students the object of the game is to make pairs and be the first to run out of cards. Have one student in each group shuffle the cards and deal five cards to each player. Invite students to try to form pairs from the cards in their hand and place pairs on the table. Invite the first student in each group to look at his or her hand and choose a card to try to match. For example, a student with the crayon card asks another student in the group *Do you have any /long a/ cards in your hand?* If he or she has the card, it is given to the student asking for it. If not, the player asking has to *go fish* by drawing the top card off the remaining pile. Play continues until all of the cards have been matched.

- Flashing Phonemes—Photocopy, cut apart, and distribute to each student the letter cards for the vowel sound you want students to review. Photocopy the corresponding picture cards on overhead transparencies. Cut the transparencies into individual picture cards for your own use. Have students lay the letter cards faceup on their desk. Display a picture card on an overhead projector, say the name of the picture aloud, and ask students to hold up the matching letter card for the vowel sound heard at the beginning of the word. This can also be done for the middle or end of the word.

- Folder Sorts—Write on the tab of a folder vowel sounds for students to review, and open the folder lengthwise. Glue matching letter cards across the top of the folder, one picture card under each letter card, and an envelope on the outside of the folder. Cut out the remaining picture cards, and store them in the envelope. Invite students to take the picture cards from the envelope and sort them in the appropriate column. Have students show you their work when they are done, and discuss with them the choices they made. Make additional picture cards for extended practice.

- Phoneme Mobile—Photocopy the picture cards for the vowel sounds you want students to review. Distribute a hanger, string or yarn, picture cards, and the corresponding letter cards to each student. Invite students to match each picture card to the appropriate letter card, color the cards, punch a hole in the top and bottom of each card, and string each vowel group along one piece of string or yarn. Finally, have students tie the strings to the hanger and decorate it with more string or yarn.

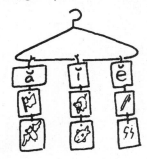

- Letter Book—Photocopy and cut apart the picture and letter cards for the two vowels on which you want students to focus. Punch a hole in the top corners of each card. Invite students to sort the cards and color them to make a book. Have students thread pipe cleaners through the holes in the cards to hold the book together.

- Room Search—Photocopy and cut apart picture cards for the vowel sounds on which you want students to focus. Hide them around the room, and invite students to try to find matching pairs. Have students who found cards for the same sound, such as the *ar* cards, gather in one spot or be in a cooperative group for that day.

- Mystery Necklace—Photocopy and cut apart the picture cards for all the vowel sounds. Punch holes in the top and bottom center of each one, and string together the cards with the same vowel sounds on a yard (meter) length of yarn to make a "necklace." Place a necklace on each student so that the cards are worn on his or her

back. Then, invite students to circulate, read each other's cards, and give each other clues to help guess what vowel sound they have. Suggest that students offer other words that contain the same vowel sound to give clues without telling the actual picture on the card.

- Flash Cards—Photocopy and cut apart the picture cards for several vowel sounds. Write the vowel sound represented by each picture on the back of each card, and invite students to use the cards as flash cards. Have students look at each picture card, say the name of the picture, decide which vowel sound is heard in that word, and check the back for accuracy.

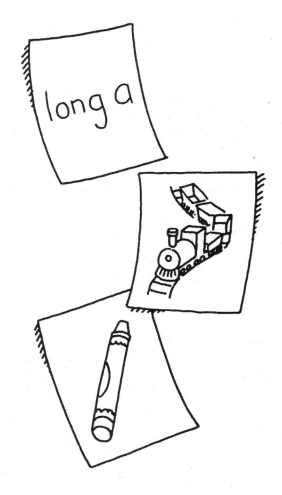

Picture Cards: short *a*

short a

Picture Cards: short *i*

short i

Picture Cards: short o

short o

Picture Cards: short e

short e

Phonics Without Worksheets: Vowels © 1999 Creative Teaching Press

Picture Cards: short *u*

short u		

Picture Cards: *ea/ee*

long e

Phonics Without Worksheets: Vowels © 1999 Creative Teaching Press

Picture Cards: *oa/ue*

Picture Cards: *ai/ay*

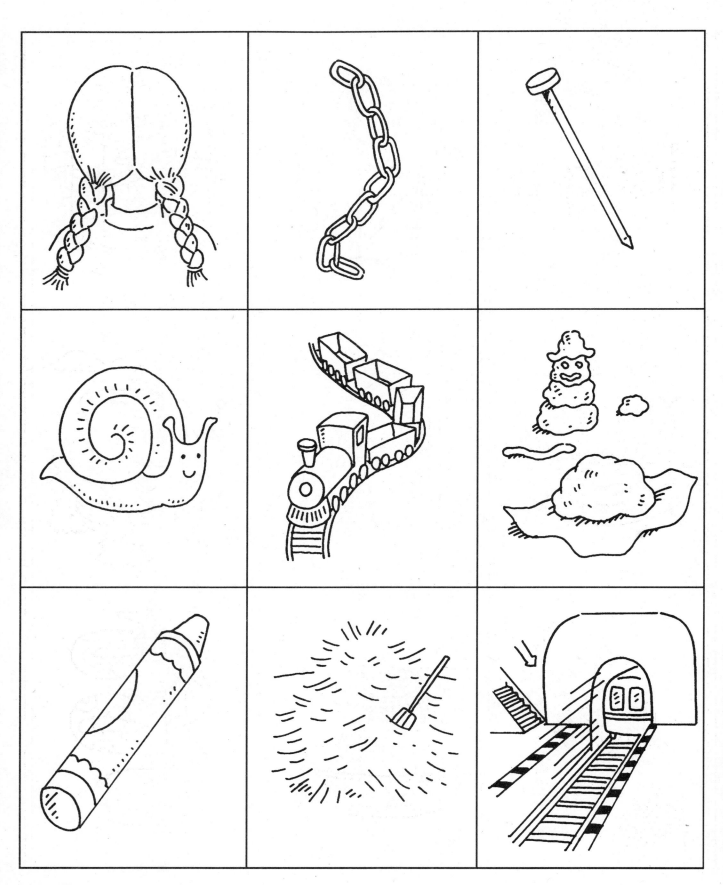

Phonics Without Worksheets: Vowels © 1999 Creative Teaching Press

Picture Cards: silent *e* with *a*

long a

Picture Cards: silent *e* with *i*

long i

Phonics Without Worksheets: Vowels © 1999 Creative Teaching Press

Picture Cards: silent *e* with *o*

long o

Picture Cards: silent *e* with *u*

long u

Phonics Without Worksheets: Vowels © 1999 Creative Teaching Press

Picture Cards: *r*-controlled words

ar		
er		
ir		

Picture Cards: *r*-controlled words

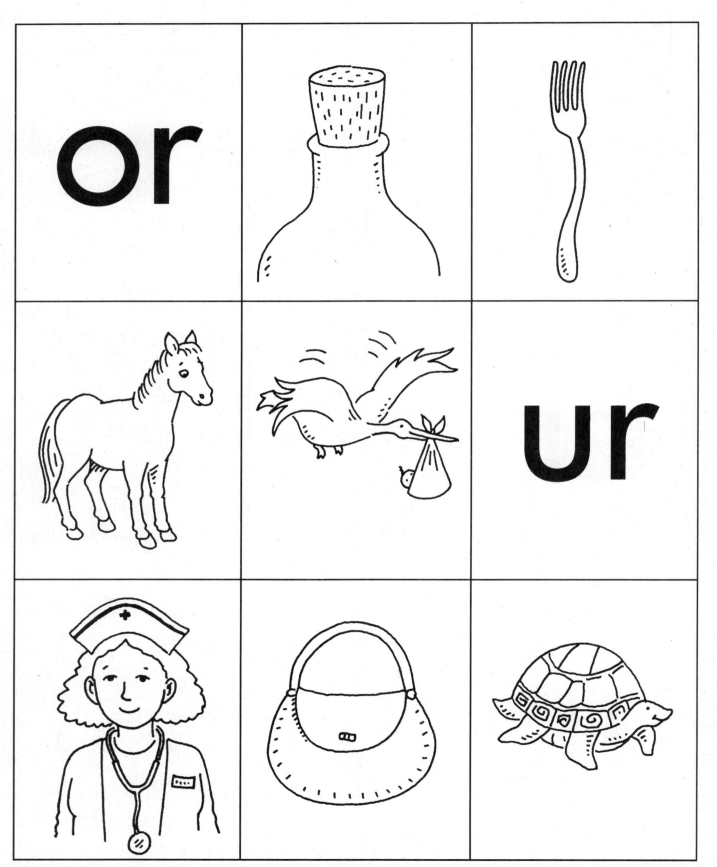